SOLO PLUS
Trumpet
with piano accompaniment

An outstanding collection from the standards & jazz repertoire expertly arranged
for the beginning soloist with piano accompaniment
in printed *and* digitally recorded formats.

Cover photography by Randall Wallace

This book Copyright © 1998 by Amsco Publications,
A Division of Music Sales Corporation, New York

All rights reserved. No part of this book may be
reproduced in any form or by any electronic or mechanical means,
including information storage and retrieval systems,
without permission in writing from the publisher.

Order No. AM 947507
US International Standard Book Number: 0.8256.1668.1
UK International Standard Book Number: 0.7119.6958.2

Exclusive Distributors:
Music Sales Corporation
257 Park Avenue South, New York, NY 10010 USA
Music Sales Limited
8/9 Frith Street, London W1V 5TZ England
Music Sales Pty. Limited
120 Rothschild Street, Rosebery, Sydney, NSW 2018, Australia

Printed in the United States of America by
Vicks Lithograph and Printing Corporation

Amsco Publications
New York/London/Sydney

Contents

Title	Solo	Accompaniment	CD Track
Angel Eyes	4	6	2
Anthropology	16	45	14
Blood Count	14	38	12
Bouncin' With Bud	3	3	1
But Beautiful	5	9	3
Darn That Dream	7	15	5
Here's That Rainy Day	11	28	8
Imagination	8	18	6
In Walked Bud	6	12	4
Ladybird	10	24	5
Like Someone In Love	12	30	10
Polka Dots And Moonbeams	15	42	13
Ruby, My Dear	9	21	7
Swinging On A Star	13	34	11

Bouncin' With Bud

Moderately fast swing (♩ = 138)

by Earl 'Bud' Powell and Walter 'Gil' Fuller

Copyright © 1947 (Renewed) by Embassy Music Corporation (BMI) and Music Sales Corporation (ASCAP)
All rights outside the U.S. controlled by Music Sales Corporation
International Copyright Secured. All Rights Reserved.

Angel Eyes

by Matt Dennis and Earl Brent

Slow and bluesy (♩ = 56)

But Beautiful

by Johnny Burke and Jimmy Van Heusen

In Walked Bud

by Thelonious Monk

Moderately fast swing (♩ = 160)

13

Darn That Dream

Moderately slow swing (♩ = 76)

by Jimmy Van Heusen and Edgar De Lange

Imagination

by Johnny Burke and Jimmy Van Heusen

Easy swing (♩ = 112)

Copyright © 1939 (Renewed) by Music Sales Corporation (ASCAP) and Bourne Co.
International Copyright Secured. All Rights Reserved.

20

Ruby, My Dear

by Thelonious Monk

Ladybird

by Tadd Dameron

Moderate swing (♩ = 138)

Here's That Rainy Day

by Johnny Burke and Jimmy Van Heusen

Like Someone In Love

by Johnny Burke and Jimmy Van Heusen

Swinging On A Star

by Johnny Burke and Jimmy Van Heusen

Blood Count

by Billy Strayhorn

Copyright © 1967 (Renewed) by Music Sales Corporation and Tempo Music, Inc.
All Rights Administered by Music Sales Corporation (ASCAP)
International Copyright Secured. All Rights Reserved.

Polka Dots And Moonbeams

by Johnny Burke and Jimmy Van Heusen

Moderate swing (♩ = 80)

44

Anthropology

by Dizzy Gillespie and Charles Parker

Bright swing (♩ = 144)